ONLINE COURSE GUIDE FOR INSTRUCTORS

COMPREHENSIVE GUIDE FOR PREPARING ONLINE COURSES, UNDERSTANDING STUDENTS, MANAGING COURSE SUBSCRIBERS AND ONLINE TEACHING STRATEGY FOR INSTRUCTORS

GARY BRADSON

This book or any portion thereof may not be reproduced or used in any manner whatsoever without the express written permission of the publisher except for the use of brief quotations in a book review.

You are welcome to join the

<u>Fan's Corner, here</u>

Online Course Guide for Instructors

Comprehensive Guide for Preparing Online Courses, Understanding Students, Managing Course Subscribers and Online Teaching Strategy for Instructors

Gary Bradson

Disclaimer

The advice and strategies found within may not be suitable for every situation. This work is sold with the understanding that neither the author nor the publisher is held responsible for the results accrued from the advice in this book.

TABLE OF CONTENT

INTRODUCTION

An online form of education is increasingly becoming a preferred form of training platform, by a lot of individuals who may not be able to attend traditional brick and mortar kind of classes for various reasons.

Anyone who is able to provide these forms of online teaching will soon find that he has more demand for services than he may struggle to manage, which is why a good book like this is needed to help you prepare and manage the process from conception, technology, and actual teaching.

Because of the freedom that can be associated with online classes, people are no longer bound by location or travel restrictions to be able to attend courses anywhere in the world even if they do not have a visa to physically attend, but for them to find your course suitable for their needs, there are things that you have to be in place as the instructor or educator.

This book was designed with the instructor in mind to help him or she be a better course provider. It does this by showing the different online teaching strategies that you can utilize for your effective content delivery and presentation.

You will also be shown a few online platforms that you can use whether or not your course content is a regular subject content, a specific career course, a fitness course, life coaching, or many other applications that you may want to apply your knowledge to.

Because we know that your area of specialization may mostly be in your field of study, we have therefore taken it upon us to find out the different technologies you can deploy to make the content delivery seamless. You will find in this book, guides to ensure you prepare engaging content that will keep your students motivated throughout the course.

The use of Learning Management Systems (LMS) will also be encouraged so that you can better handle the course progress of the students, manage timelines, mark assignments, and ensure that every student has a dashboard where their progress can be seen at a glance.

With the use of your course after you follow the recommendations in this book, students will no longer miss a thing about their hitherto traditional classroom scenarios.

CHAPTER 1

AN OVERVIEW OF ONLINE TEACHING

The conventional classroom isn't the only place where students learn anymore. The educational environment has evolved into online teaching which makes it possible for students to learn from the comfort of their homes, and any other place convenient for them.

Recent research has shown that students that learn online perform satisfactorily on average than those who learn in conventional institutions. Online classes have been able to allow students to participate wherever at their own comfort regardless of terrain, income, or society. These online classes when deployed effectively can conform and even outperform the classroom education.

Key aspects of teaching online

To improve online teaching and create a thriving fundamental learning program to encourage instructors and learners to grow, certain vital aspects of online teaching are required.

1. **Establish a supportive online setting:** A supportive environment requires student-student relations and teacher-student arrangement. The best ways to achieve a supportive environment online is to:

- Build an outlet or forum where students can acquire support from each other and get assistance from each other.

- At the beginning of the online course, introduce yourself, and encourage students to introduce themselves as well.

2. **Establish your physical presence online:** Appearing visible to students will boost a healthy learning atmosphere. This shows that you're visible and they will become more confident and increase their desire to participate when they see you.

3. **Use learning tools**: Technology has made it easier for us to organize a

fundamental learning ground that lets us collaborate and engage just like being in the classroom. Considerable use of online learning tools boosts learners' attention.

4. **Providing quality feedback:** Providing feedback is really a key aspect of online learning because feedback is a crucial element for effective learning both online and offline. Feedback will help to build experiences that engage learners and create a feeling of community in an online class.

5. **Create offline e-learning content:** This is really a great option as it allows students to learn offline. It gives them

access to the materials which boosts their growth, and progress. You can develop offline learning content by giving offline assignments (like writing answers to questions). Offline learning strategy is a great aspect that allows learners to learn how to make better decisions and work better on their own without depending on other students.

6. **Create live conferences:** An offline session is necessary for facilitating students' performances. This can be in the form of dividing students into small groups for mentoring or mentoring individually at scheduled times. Live

meetings are really helpful in dealing with gaps in learning, facilitates in-depth understanding and feedbacks.

THE CHANGING FACE OF THE EDUCATIONAL ENVIRONMENT

An online class is a potential form of learning platform that is effective in providing an alternative practices and activities for learning. To appropriately utilize this powerful setting, a coordinated, validating, and cooperative learning atmosphere must be created and the technology to be deployed in this form of teaching should be fully understood by tutors to ensure students enjoy the advantages of the online class.

Here are the basic reasons why the educational environment is changing.

1. **The need to cut costs:** Cutting costs has become a great factor resulting in the inception of online programs. Conventional institutions are influenced as a means to counteract for overfilled classes, and a strategy to save costs. The online learning program has the tendency to be impressively personalized for each learner and bring better results than the traditional one at similar rates or even lower.

2. **The desire for flexibility and personalized learning:** Flexibility is

crucial in modern-day education as not everyone can leave work to learn full time in school. The online class has been able to offer flexibility for individuals to acquire knowledge at their convenience and their own pace.

3. **The need for control:** The educational environment has been evolving to suit students and give them the ability to have more control over what and how they learn.

PRINCIPLES OF EFFECTIVE ONLINE TEACHING

Effective online teaching blends both the strategies for supporting learners with the perception of course design

1. Effective online teachers are present and accessible

In online learning, students need to know they have a teacher who attends to them, is present to support them, and makes them feel like they are part of an active learning community. Effective online teachers create their presence and accessibility during the course and after lessons. This communication creates a relationship that is based on trust and confidence, which is the basis of the learning process.

2. Effective online teachers apply appropriate methods to facilitate student success while recognizing institutional drawbacks

Students find fulfillment in their learning process when they can relate to the teacher, and when learning goals and the lesson content relates to their familiar and personal experiences. Assigning proper and suitable techniques for the success of the students. This principle recognizes learning obstacles and drawbacks in the online learning setting and introduces significant practices to promote fair results across disciplines. This principle enables:

- Creating culturally aware course content and analysis,

- Promoting students as they steer towards expectations of the system while improving their digital literacy;

- Cultivating students' sense of cooperation and an increase in active engagement;

- Establishing potential for creating equity-minded institutions;

- Mapping out online teaching and learning goals and plans

3. Effective online teachers are responsive to the needs of the student and use data for steady course modification.

Effective teaching is generally dynamic. Whenever you teach a course, present a lecture, or engage your students in a learning activity, you teach when you answer to student questions and give constructive feedback. Effective teachers use the experience to revise a lesson from one term to another term. Great online courses are not just barely copied from term to term without substantial modifications, but instead are taught actively and modified.

This principle enables the online teacher to:

- Connect students' self-assessment to direct learning opportunities

- Utilize constructive and effective assessment and course analytics to track student interaction, learning, and appropriate response

- Effectively using communication tools to connect with the student and ensure their success

- Constantly formulating plans for modifying lessons

4. Effective online teachers teach and form an ethical online relationship while helping students improve digital literacy that will prepare them for success

In recent times, students will be greatly successful if they have digital confidence that facilitates their distinct capacities and potential. Online teachers ought to prepare to play an important part in the advancement of their students' digital presence. Students aspire to be like their instructors who industriously design careful and proficient use of digital tools and resources.

Effective online teachers fully realize that engaging students online is a significant part of becoming literate digitally and as such, learning is not just based on a textbook.

This principle places emphasis on:

- Improving one's own professional digital presence

- Cultivating a learning doctrine that promotes interest and critical assessment of online resources while promoting digital literacy

- Creating opportunities for students to develop content that can be shared outside of a learning system

- Promoting a learning environment that motivates students to relate with and learn from a universal audience

5. Effective online instructors understand ongoing professional development is a fundamental factor in their success

Technology is dynamic, our perception of the most beneficial and constructive means to connect with students is a primary aspect of practical online teaching and must be a continuous improvement professional development.

COMMON MYTHS ABOUT ONLINE TEACHING

Some online education misconceptions are widespread. When online learning was first recommended as a feasible option for in-class learning, many people were hesitant and doubtful. And, at the time, their skepticisms were understood.

Unfortunately, even though the condition of online learning has tremendously improved and advanced over the years, yet, many of these initial misconceptions have yet to disappear.

Below are some of the myths several people have about online education, and why they're either not authentic, or detailed enough.

1. Online classes aren't as effective as conventional classroom learning

There are numerous inferior online courses, just as there are low and poor classroom experiences. The platform used to convey the class lesson is almost as significant as how it's implemented and assessed. Over time, several online courses have showed themselves to be just as productive as their conventional counterparts when it comes to teaching and learning.

Online education uses the advantages of analytics methods and tools to help instructors identify difficult parts in their classes. Consequently, online courses have developed rapidly, and are now satisfying and matching choices to physical classroom courses.

2. Online classes are easier than in conventional classes

Online classes are not easier in comparison to conventional classes because online classes are usually more rigorous and demanding and require more time. Thorough reading conditions and critical time management for assignment deadlines are needed for the success of the students in an online class. A few students register for online classes with the assumption that they will be able to cruise through the lessons. However, anyone who has ever collected a take-home assignment will know that instructors often try to balance the availability of materials by increasing expectations and goals.

Online classes are also time demanding just like classroom lessons. They often contain additional composed correspondence with teachers and classmates, and also additional tests, examinations, quizzes, or coursework that are written to assess progress. Students who overlook the activity take the risk of lagging behind. Therefore, underestimating the time commitment is not a good idea

3. That Online courses are not accredited

Ever since online schooling became more popular and accepted, many accredited institutions have incorporated online lessons as an aspect of their curriculum. In fact, it is uncommon for many recent university students to graduate without ever having taken an online class. But it's not just higher education that provides the accredited course. More private instructors are taking steps to obtain accreditation for their online classes, thereby improving its integrity and significance. Also, the paths these teachers need to go with to gain accreditation are stressful, this is like an indication that because it's online doesn't mean it's simple to use.

4. Employers or academic establishments do not regard online courses

An issue with this misconception is that it attends all online courses like they are all the same. Though some online courses are not respectable, then, some institutions are also not reputable. The student is expected to research and investigate before deciding if a course is worth the effort or not. Well, the increasing figures of accredited online courses bring thriving integrity and approval among employers and educational institutions. Some companies even expect an actual online certificate as an aspect of employee growth. As for academic establishments, students who intend to transfer must always do a review with the college or university to see if their credits will be carried over or not. This is true of online and conventional class credits alike.

5. You can cheat easily in an online course.

Online cheating was a crucial problem for a long time, but technology has developed and helped to deal with this problem. The use of features such as browser blocking functions during test periods to keystroke tracking, most online courses have better cheat-proof features than physical classrooms. Online schooling also tends to assess and examine students differently. When the lesson requires communication in-class meetings, frequent micro-quizzes, or even video exhibitions, discovering means to cheat can constantly become more of a nuisance than just performing the course task.

6. Online students don't communicate with the instructor

Students can have a great relationship with their teachers even more than a conventional classroom setting. Some online classes have required "log-on" times or mandatory contributions in chat rooms and on discussion boards. This helps to develop a sense of relationship in the online class setting. Students can still contact instructors. Though this depends on the educator. There are courses where the educator just teaches in the background setting and students practically follow the procedure and memorize on their own. However, online class platforms also allow instructors to partake in conversations and discussions and chat forums, live webinars, or also perform video chats with students who need more personal guide and advice. For private instructors, these are also outstanding service that can be used to increase the value of the course. Online classes create an important community of learners.

7. Online courses do not give room for interaction with fellow students

It's factual that many online students feel more disconnected and isolated than learning in physical classes. Nevertheless, this is usually the outcome of the course design, rather than an inherent shortcoming in online education. Discussion boards, online cooperative schemes, and group webinars are all constructive manners in which fellow students can converse and relate to each other during an online lesson. While it can be uneasy for students to start the conversation, with the right encouragement most students find confidence expressing themselves in writing than in speaking. This may make online schooling a safe and easy way for introverts to unite and interact with their online classmates than in conventional classrooms.

8. You have to possess computer literacy

It's difficult to say how valid this misconception may be because being proficient in computer literacy can differ greatly from user to user. In one perspective a "computer person" is an individual who writes code for a living. From another perspective, even simple interactions on a computer are unfamiliar and unusual. That said, several online instructors have worked to develop accessible, user-friendly online courses, with the purpose of developing an automatic interface that doesn't disrupt the learning process. This implies that the majority of online education classes need little or no special computer skills.

9. You can do assignments anytime

Students can complete their assignments anytime whether day or night, but assignments must be submitted by the deadline given for submitting the assignment. Browse the class syllabus for the roster of assignments and deadlines.

10. Online classes do not observe the regular semester routine

Online lessons observe the same academic calendar as an offline class. Fees, scheduling, systems for withdrawing, and other protocols are similar for online classes.

11. You can stay unidentified in an online class

There are tons of required interactions and activities between students and instructors in an online class. This gives room for an opportunity for students to relate with each other, engage in conversations and dialogue. Since these meetings are not face-to-face, it enables timid individuals to partake in a relaxing atmosphere.

12.   Broken and damaged computers are reasonable excuses

A damaged or broken computer is not a justifiable and reasonable explanation for a missed deadline. There are several alternatives available to back up assignments and tasks. Most online instructors will not accept the explanation that a computer was broken or damaged. A serious and devoted student can always get a computer device to continue his work. Planning for unforeseen circumstances and careful thoughts are expected in an online class, and that includes making sure the student gains access to a computer and Internet connection when it's time to finish assignments.

13.   It's okay to procrastinate in online courses

Procrastination is not accepted nor encouraged. Procrastination in an online class can result in additional challenges for students than procrastination in a conventional class. Online students are expected to be self-sufficient, inspired, and independent. Students should be able to establish and observe their own plans and schedules. Students need to be able to manage the flexibility of an online class.

## 14.	Instructors provide computer instructions

Instructors don't give instructions on how to use a computer or give technological assistance or illustrate computer usage in addition to teaching the class lesson. If the class needs to use sophisticated software the educator will make sure students get instructions on how to use that specialized software. Students should possess computer skills before joining an online class.

## 15.	You can cram all your work into one login session

It is hard for students to be successful in learning when they hardly log in. Most students comprehend best when they get an opportunity to learn in smaller doses of information, then analyze that material content learning more. Furthermore, many instructors expect a regular contribution to online discussions. Not only does this interaction help students appreciate new ideas and opinions, sometimes credits and grade points are given for active class participation. Grades can be static if students log in only once every week or two.

CHAPTER 2

STRATEGIES FOR MANAGING YOUR ONLINE COURSE

Online classes are great but also come with their challenges. An excellent management strategy in place is necessary to motivate your students, achieve better results, and boost the success of your online program.

1. **Active communication:** The educational environment has changed so much that personal connection is essential for online programs. A standard communication platform motivates the students and establishes a perception of normalcy. Zoom is one of the best

communication platforms you can use. Human connection is an essential requirement to help students stay motivated.

2. **Engaging students:** Priorities generally change in online teaching and lack of connection makes students lose interest. You would agree with me that students can get bored listening to a 5-hour lecture every day, but engaging students by introducing activities and problem-solving tasks makes students learn better than assimilating knowledge. This works even with offline classrooms, so engaging your

students is a wonderful option for keeping them focused.

3. **Develop student decision-making process:** Student decision making is a significant aspect of online student management because even though you can provide students with preferences and varieties of knowledge to learn from, you aren't accountable for their learning. Student ownership includes allowing students formulate their goals and allowing them to make decisions about their learning process. Ensure they write down their goals and create steps to achieve that goal. Give room for errors

and mistakes and inquire guiding questions to help them achieve their goals.

4. **Begin gradually:** Allow students to gradually adjust to the online learning process as the new norm. You can make this adjustment by having a reduced task you assign to a students at the beginning and then gradually increase that as the weeks progresses. Use the initial week to focus on the systems of online learning, keep it entertaining, simple, and supporting, and then you can increase your pace later on.

5. **Create standards and principles:** As one would expect to find, institutions and

any organization should have a set of rules to enable it to run smoothly and it serves as a guide to your students. Standards can be as simple as defining when they can ask questions, proper outfit for online conferences, principles for cooperative documents. It's also great to allow your students to be involved in deciding what the rules should be, through collaborative ideas and suggestions as they will be more likely to conform to the rules if they are involved.

MANAGING YOUR STUDENT'S BEHAVIOR

Productive teachers use several strategies to manage the behaviors of their students, therefore it's crucial to create rules and expectations to guide their behaviors.

1. **Set behavioral expectations:** You can set behavioral expectations and review before you begin the classes and this can be in the form of clues, and constructive narrative. Yes, you can also use incentives to enhance behavioral expectations. Allow your students to engage in conversation with you, their learning environment, and their fellow students.

2. **Have a positive attitude:** A positive attitude has proven to be tremendously

effective than penalty because students prefer friendly teachers. You can also apply the principle of being strict and friendly at different times depending on the occasion. So, a positive and friendly atmosphere makes your class interesting to students and influences your students' attitude to learn.

3. **Carry your students along:** A great way to manage the behavior of your students is to make sure you update them as you go with the lesson, and make sure none of them feels left out, this will increase their participation. Also, encourage them to ask questions, give

group projects to cultivate the spirit of cooperation among them. Maintain a track of the active students and encourage the inactive students to partake more.

4. **Address indiscipline instantly**: Addressing acts of indiscipline will create a balance in your class. Keep a constructive mood even when correcting students, and encourage them to improve their attitude. Learn how to handle different situations like interruptions, offensive languages, and other issues.

5. **Praise your students:** As with a lot of other aspects of life, positive comments about an individual motivates that

individual. It also applies to online classes, praising your students as their performances improves or as they make progress is a way to motivate them to do more. A reward system is an excellent way to show your students that you recognize their performances.

6. **Create a routine:** A class routine process is an excellent way to make your student comfortable. They know what they should expect when they progress and your reaction to unacceptable behaviors. Ensure you observe the routine to make the study process more effective.

TIME MANAGEMENT

Effective time management is an important technique that makes it easy for you to accomplish your goals and objectives. As an educator, you may be overpowered by the pressures of teaching online, realizing that there is no exact duration of hours for the course and it's open 24 hours a day and 7 days a week.

Having an effective way to manage your time can have a great impact on your productivity as well as your health. Some suggested ways of effectively managing your time can include:

1. **Schedule your time teaching activities every week:** You should schedule your time into your calendar, this can be a 1, 2 or 3-hour time period

for evaluating learners, you can do this weekly to give you time for other things.

2. **Create a valuable grading system:** Grading can be time-consuming if you're trying to give quality evaluation and positive feedback because it's important for your online class. You can decide to get a program like a screencast program for providing feedback whether written or verbal. This makes it easier for you and saves you time. Get efficient grading devices to grade assignments.

3. **Let your students evaluate each other's work:** You can divide your class into small groups, give an assignment,

allow them to interact, and rate each other's conversation at the end of a particular time.

4. **Be organized:** Organization is crucial to an online teacher whether you take 1 or 5 courses. Use pads, teachers' planning books, rosters, reminders, and various time management tools to organize your activities.

5. **Plan for unexpected occurrence:** Situations we don't plan for at times may arise when we least expect, no matter how cautious we may be, or how sensibly we plan. This may be technical complications, or, shortage of supplies,

students who need assistance, etc. Map out a plan for unseen or unexpected situations, they help you tackle that situation better.

LEGAL AND ETHICAL ISSUES MANAGEMENT

With a blend of technology and education, a few challenges will arise because modern laws are drafted each year. Ethical issues are prevalent in online programs. Some of the challenges you may encounter are:

1. **Intellectual property and copyright issues:** If you use content already made by someone you will need to seek

permission before you can use the material to avoid copyright theft.

2. **Online harassment challenges:** Harassment online such as online bullying and cyberbullying can be managed by having identified offenders prosecuted in line with the state education law. You can create awareness through the course syllabus, ethical frame, and appropriate programs.

3. **Technological issues:** Technological issues like broken gadgets can be handled by students themselves or their parents.

4. **Ethical issues:** An instance of an ethical issue is using or buying an academic

material that is outdated or isn't correct. To be on the safe side make sure your content is updated and accredited content.

In summary, if you're faced with legal and ethical issues, you can take it to your state's education board, or you can get an academic lawyer to take it up.

DEVELOPING ONLINE TEACHING PHILOSOPHY

Online teaching philosophies reflect your virtues and principles about teaching. It reflects your values and ideas about teaching. It entails your set goals and how you intend to achieve them, examples of your teaching styles and inquiry method, what you believe in when you come to teach. A teaching philosophy can more or less be like a preamble to your teaching portfolio and a means of professional development.

HOW TO DEVELOP YOUR ONLINE TEACHING PHILOSOPHY

Note that an online teaching philosophy should be in a narrative form and highly engaging, summarized, written in a first-person and optimistic tone, states goal, teaching, and methods, can also include experience if you wish.

Before developing your online teaching, you should answer these questions:

1. What are your concepts when it comes to learning?

2. What do you want to leave with your students after each class?

3. What motivates you to teach?

4. What is a real or ideal teaching situation for you?

5. What are your goals as a teacher?

6. What are your goals for each class?

7. What are your teaching strategies?

8. How would you mentor students?

9. What is your grading and assessment method?

10. How do you intend to achieve your set goals?

These questions above are your guide to developing your own online teaching philosophy.

HOW TO MANAGE FAILING STUDENTS

Managing a failing student can be difficult because failing students can make you worried and frustrated, worse still it leaves you not knowing what to do. As an online instructor, you have an obligation to help your struggling student succeed and make progress. Here are some strategies that you can use to help your struggling and failing students.

1. **Know the underlying problems behind their failure:** The best and easiest way to help a student is to understand the reasons behind such a failure. You can know this reason by interacting with the student, observing the student's behavior. When you have successfully identified the reasons behind

the student falling behind, you can then create a solution appropriate to the situation, this can be in the form of extra classes, probationary period, medical treatment, or some period to rest.

2. **Build strong and reliable foundations:** Have compulsory tips and tricks sessions to help students embrace online learning, offer tutorials before you begin the course to help the students become exposed to online learning.

3. **Motivate them:** Yes, struggling and failing students also feel frustrated and discouraged. You need to encourage them as much as you can by praising them and

making them know that you believe in them and as such, they also need to believe in themselves. Encourage their tiniest progress.

4. **Make your course easy for comprehension:** Start your courses with simple ideas and break down your chapters, make your assignments easy to boost your students' confidence.

5. **Track their progress:** You can track your student's progress through assessments and tests to see how far they understand, give corrections where there are errors and feedbacks.

6. **Be accessible to them:** Offer ways and platforms for students struggling to get access to you, this makes it easier for them to feel carried along, create a chat forum or discussion board, so they can interact with other students.

Believe in them, don't give up on them, you may achieve your results in the long run, you can help your struggling students with these strategies and make them have a more satisfying learning experience.

CHAPTER 3

CONNECTING AND COMMUNICATING WITH STUDENTS

The educating environment is fast changing as the online learning environment is already a part of the system, new learning tools are out, more and more students are taking online courses. It is required of an online instructor to create an environment where the students can feel connected.

While it is possible for you to see your online students as just usernames, grading, and as a to-do list task, a strong connection with your student is crucial as this makes them communicate meaningfully and sparks up their interest, motivates them and increases their chances of success. Here are a few easy and effective strategies you can use to create connections with online students.

1. **Facilitating discussions through online community**: Develop an online community where students can post questions and hold discussions. You can also talk about yourself by posting useful and some personal information about yourself. At the early stage of your course you can also encourage introductory statements by creating introductory videos to welcome them to the course and use the opportunity to introduce yourself. This is an effective way to engage with

your students as they can then see you as a human being behind the scene and not a virtual robot.

2. **Provide Feedback:** Feedbacks are a great option when it comes to interacting with your students. Feedback helps students know where their errors and helps them improve, use emails, chats, announcements, and discussion forums to provide feedback to students. Additionally, personal feedback feels more private and works even better. A screencast can be used to create audiovisual feedbacks.

3. **Create videos:** Creating an online presence with videos is an effective way to connect with your students. Use videos for brief lectures, welcome messages, and announcements. Make the video original, unique, and simple, simple actions like these can help make your students feel connected to you.

4. **Communication:** Use communication platforms to connect with your students. Ensure your students uses the communication outlet. You can connect with communication tools such as emails, forums, announcements, course calendars, podcasts, interactive sessions,

webcasts, activities, online office hours, video messages and calls.

5. **Make them a part of the decision-making process:** Giving students a chance to make choices, engages them, and builds a strong connection with you. Give them a choice of topics and projects. Make a variety of choices for them to choose from.

6. **Reward them:** Rewards will motivate students, and keep them committed to learning. Effective instructors use rewards to keep their students' learning interests. Rewards make your students connected to

you and propels them to work harder to increase their performances.

CHANNELS OF COMMUNICATION FOR YOUR ONLINE CLASS

Communication skill is an excellent skill that will go a long way in determining the success of your online class. Technology has even made it easier for communications between individuals and communities, though it can be challenging, but if you concentrate on adopting technology, you can achieve great results. Communication keeps you in touch with your students. Here are communication channels you need for your class;

Videos: Videos are great communication tools and there are good media channels like YouTube, periscope and a few others that you can use when sharing them. You can also do live streaming, students can connect easily to you when they see and hear you.

Audio conferencing: Audio conferencing is an easy way to pass messages or info to your students. Endeavor to keep the audio message clear and concise.

Text messages: Text messages are efficient communication tools especially when you have a piece of vital information to deliver to the entire class.

Emails: Email makes it easy for students and guardians to contact you directly. Email is one of the simplest methods that students can get to you directly with.

Social media and mobile apps: Apps like Skype and Zoom make it easy for you and your students to communicate with each other, they provide voice chats like you are using a phone.

Live chat sessions are also great ways for students to voice their issues. Voicing out private issues may not be recommended with this channel but it's a great method.

Other tips for effective communications are:

i. Your message should be understandable and concise.

ii. A bulk of text can be boring, use bullet points and lists to deliver your message.

iii. Make use of private communication for delicate and sensitive messages to develop trust, safety, and privacy in the online learning atmosphere.

iv.   Use appropriate and suitable vocabulary and grammar.

v.   Make communication personal by identifying the names of students to create familiarity and connection.

CHAPTER 4

SCAFFOLDING, DEVELOPING COGNITIVE AND SOCIAL STRATEGIES

SCAFFOLDING

Scaffolding includes the various methods that are taken to promote students' progress to boost their knowledge and comprehension and ensure they achieve independence in the process of learning. It is a vital factor in teaching and requires a lot of efforts to provide support to students to enable them to gain greater understanding and skill.

Generally, these supporting processes are aborted once the desired results are achieved and the student can learn independently. Most instructors to an extent use scaffolding in their teaching because of how important it is in effective teaching. Scaffolding is one of the precepts of practical teaching that helps teachers to accommodate the needs of every student.

The major aim of scaffolding is to try to push students to do better, achieve learning expectations or milestones, and bridge learning gaps. It also aims at reducing negative feelings that a student may feel when they are depressed or demoralized. Scaffolding helps students to become self-sufficient, self-reliant and increases their problem-solving ability.

This strategy builds on the initial knowledge of students with the use of materials, tools, and technology to support the learners' activities. In scaffolding, teachers show how to solve a problem and then step back from giving the students too much help or attention, although students with slower learning assimilation may be given more attention and the opportunity to improve at a slower pace.

A few examples, of scaffolding strategies can include a teacher with a difficult lesson breaking them down into series of easy mini bits, and then progressively increasing the difficulty level so the student can have a strong foundation of that concept. Another instance is using various means to illustrate a lesson. This could be in the form of images or videos to make the student articulate the lesson and deepen their understanding. Teachers can also give a vocabulary lesson before giving the assignment to make them relate to the assignment easily.

TYPES OF SCAFFOLDING

Procedural Scaffolding

Procedural scaffolding involves allowing students to use available tools. It makes the lesson easily comprehendible by using available resources, tools, and support before and after the lesson. This scaffold facilitates the student's learning and language acquisition. An example, of a procedural scaffold, is asking supportive open-ended questions, graphic representation, text charts and navigation maps.

Conceptual Scaffolding

Conceptual scaffolding assists students in choosing what to consider during learning and guides to value basic concepts.

Strategic scaffolding

Strategic scaffolding help learners find techniques to solve challenging issues.

Metacognitive scaffolding

Metacognitive scaffolding is an intended instruction or dealing developed particularly to promote students' understanding of metacognitive strategies.

Synergetic scaffolding –This involves using a different type of technique to a similar problem. For example, a rise in health problems during rain, a change in wall color, difference in the color drinking water, all of these all focus on one major issue of pollution.

Differentiated scaffolding – This is an essential type of scaffolding that can be significantly used to think back to the previously learned lesson or make connections between the previously learned concepts. This can also be graphics based, number games or word games, poems, or literary activities that can also be used in this type.

An effective scaffolding results in an excellent experience. Here are effective strategies that you can use in scaffolding.

SCAFFOLDING STRATEGIES

1. TEACH VOCABULARY BEFORE LESSONS

This is an effective strategy that teachers don't maximize to the fullest. Letting students go through a road filled with words or terms that may be difficult to understand isn't ideal. This can make them confused and lose interest in the whole thing before it even begins.

Teaching your students vocabulary involves introducing the words to them in connection with things they are interested in and also familiar with. Allow them to talk about the word and then further use a dictionary to explain the word. This makes them ready to tackle and difficult words.

2. USE GRAPHICS AND VISIBLE DIAGRAMS TO TEACH

You can use graphics, images, diagrams, and maps as excellent scaffolding tools. Graphics helps to picture ideas visibly their ideas and capture ideas like cause and effect. This is an effective strategy that helps fashion how students think. Yes, some students can easily compose a piece or even draft a theory without using a graphic organizer but most students will gain from using a graphic organizer.

3. ASK QUESTIONS AND REVIEW

This is an amazing strategy to evaluate students' understanding. A great way to use this strategy is to share a fresh idea from a discussion, wait, and give them time to think and then ask a question. Lay out the questions early, make sure they're detailed, direct and open-ended. If the class appears to find the questions difficult, allow the students to discuss in pairs. Teachers have to discover and attempt new scaffolding strategies because of the various kinds of learners in classrooms. The outcome of scaffolding is a rewarding experience even though it takes time to impact.

4. UTILIZE INITIAL KNOWLEDGE

Allow students to share their understandings, feelings, and opinions about the subject and let them relate and connect it to their own lives. Sometimes you can offer clues and recommendations, to help them get the message. Utilizing the prior knowledge of your student is a general standard scaffolding strategy used by effective teachers.

DEVELOPING COGNITIVE AND SOCIAL STRATEGIES

The categories of learning strategies compare cognitive strategies, metacognitive strategies, and social strategies.

Cognitive Learning

Cognitive learning is a method of teaching that focuses on utilizing the brain effectively.

Cognition is the mental technique of attaining knowledge and reasoning through insights, experiences, and understanding. Cognitive learning strategies are strategies that help learners become better in learning. These reasoning maps, using hints in reading, spotting key words, self-testing, finding a new language, using visual objects to enhance memory, summarizing meaning, repetition, guessing, and suggestions. These strategies involve intentionally utilizing language to promote student learning. For example, a student memorizes new words by representing them visibly in a striking circumstance making it easier and quicker to remember these words.

Cognitive strategies are helpful tools in helping students with learning difficulties. In an online class that uses cognitive strategies, the teacher unites the gap between students and the lesson to be learned. The cognitive learning strategy strives to utilize the learning process for optimal reasoning, and understanding. Understanding the concept of cognitive learning makes it simple to sustain a lasting pattern of continual learning.

Cognitive learning is a fantastic way to attain proficiency in students. Cognitive strategies turn learning activities into a fully engaging and active process. Practicing cognitive strategies would help learners become excellent students.

Components of Cognitive Learning

Cognitive learning is directed at attaining knowledge and proficiency in the subject. The following components are essential to the cognitive learning process:

Comprehension: Cognitive learning strategies promote understanding and comprehension. The purpose of learning the subject should be understood

Memory: Cognitive learning encourages you to know the subject in detail and at an intense level. This builds a result that boosts your memory and enhances your potential to connect new information to past knowledge.

FUNCTIONS OF COGNITIVE LEARNING

Cognitive strategies provide a system for learning when an assignment is difficult to complete through a progression of steps.

A cognitive strategy supports students to develop internal schemes that help them accomplish difficult assignments. Reading comprehension is an instance where cognitive strategies are significant. A self-questioning technique can enable students to comprehend what they read.

The use of cognitive strategies can increase the efficiency with which the learner approaches a learning task. These academic tasks can include but are not limited to, remembering and applying information from course content, constructing sentences and paragraphs, editing written work, paraphrasing, and classifying information to be learned.

Cognitive learning is an engaging and active system that connects a learner's mind and perception in a constructive and long-lasting way. It educates them to maximize the full potentials of their brains, makes it simpler to relate new knowledge with standing ideas, boosts memory capacity.

Rather than emphasizing memorization like in the conventional style of learning, cognitive learning focuses on prior knowledge. It teaches them to evaluate the material and connect it with prior knowledge for better and active learning. This makes cognitive learning a practical means of acquiring knowledge and makes them better learners in the long run.

Benefits of Cognitive Learning

Cognitive learning is an important aspect of facilitating lasting learning and development in learners.

Boosts confidence: Cognitive learning can also boost confidence in a student's ability to handle difficult tasks and challenges. This is because it improves problem-solving skills and makes it simpler to comprehend new information.

Facilitate comprehension: Students learn by performing in cognitive learning. This technique makes learning engaging and promotes comprehension. Consequently, they can acquire a better comprehension of the material and its application to their life.

Facilitates constant learning: Cognitive techniques facilitate lasting learning by allowing learners to connect initial knowledge with recent information. It enables effectively incorporating both prior and recent knowledge.

Improves problem-solving skills: Problem-solving abilities are significant. The cognitive learning strategy enhances the ability to develop problem-solving abilities and apply them to every aspect of the learners' life.

Makes learning exciting: Cognitive strategies encourage learning by making learning exciting and fulfilling. This motivates students to develop a continuous passion and enthusiasm for learning.

Examples of cognitive learning

Here are examples of cognitive learning:

1. Implicit learning

Implicit learning is a kind of learning where there is no effective reason to acquire knowledge. It is a kind of random and impulsive learning because the learner isn't attentive to the learning process but still gains knowledge. Examples of this kind of learning include talking, eating and other things learned unintentionally. For instance, typing without looking at a keyboard.

2. Explicit learning

Explicit learning involves intentionally pursuing and striving for knowledge. It involves striving to become a master at a recent skill or running back to college for additional studies. Explicit learning requires intentional effort and maintained interest to obtain new proficiency. Cognitive learning provides explicit learning by offering remarkable knowledge into the topic. An example of explicit learning is enrolling in a PowerPoint course to boost presentation skills.

3. Cooperative and collaborative learning

Cooperative learning involves learning as a group or team. Learning cooperatively helps to strengthen cooperation and bring out the sufficient abilities in each participant at the event. Collaborate learning is a cognitive strategy in which an educator educates a group on how to expand their ideas on a particular skill or knowledge.

4. Discovery learning

Discovery learning involves actively searching for new insight into topics not mainly related to the learner's field through researching.

5. Substantial learning

Substantial learning happens when a person associates recent knowledge with prior knowledge. It includes sentimental, passion, and cognitive aspects. It facilitates problem-solving abilities and enhances knowledge. An example is attending an advanced management class to understand leadership better and also to become a better manager.

6. Emotional learning

This cognitive strategy enables learners to understand emotional reasoning and controlling their emotions and that of others. Emotional intelligence plays a significant role in interpersonal associations and constructive communication. For example, emotional learning helps students sustain a successful relationship within themselves.

7. Experiential learning

"Experience, they say, is the best teacher", this means people often learn best through experiences. Experiential learning is a cognitive technique that enables students to learn from their own experiences or the experiences of others around them. The value of an experience depends on their level of thought and examination and how they can connect it to previous circumstances.

8. Non-associative learning (habituation and sensitization)

Non-associative learning is further broken down into two styles, habituation and sensitization. Both of them focus on how to learn based on response to a constant impulse.

Habituation involves learning by habit. It involves a decreased response to a stimulant after prolonged exposure.

Sensitization is the opposite of habituation learning. In sensitization, the response increases with continuous exposure to the stimulant. Both types of learning are essential and can be adjusted to a vast scope of situations.

9. Receptive learning

This is a form of learning where an educator makes himself or herself visible to the students attending his lectures while lecturing on a topic. This form of receptive learning is mild for the learners because the educator participates actively more than the students.

10. Observation learning

This cognitive learning technique involves learning by imitation. Imitation is an effective learning tool, and it's common with youngsters. However, adults can also observe others to learn the techniques. For example, leadership skills can be learned by imitating leaders and practicing their habits.

THE SOCIAL LEARNING STRATEGY

Social learning is inherent to us as we all interact with each other and learn through association and observances. Therefore, social learning is seen as learning with others and learning from others. We all engage in social learning every day through the chats that we have with each other to the conferences and speeches. The concept of social interactions and association has always resulted in favorable developments and influences us greatly.

Social learning is an excellent learning strategy, especially when used in corporate training. Social learning requires an established semi-structured plan to enable cooperation among students. This can be done by creating platforms that allows for sharing of information and opinions and ideas.

Enhancing the Effectiveness of Social Learning System

Social learning works no doubts. With the help of these two concepts, we will see how the social learning system works.

Social learning theory

The social learning concept "is a learning concept and social character which proposes that characters can be obtained by being around and emulating others. It asserts that learning is a cognitive technique that takes place in a sociable context and can happen solely through observance or education. The key advocates of this theory discovered that, people learn by observing behaviors or its consequences even though learning is not constantly behavioral. Mere support does not serve when it comes to learning although it plays a crucial part in learning. It is a result of a collective influence of understanding, surroundings, and nature. It does not happen passively.

Active Learning theory

The active learning theory involves getting students to directly involve themselves in the learning process. It encourages students to be more actively involved in learning (by reading, writing, engaging in discussions and anything intellectual.)

THE BENEFITS OF SOCIAL LEARNING

Integrating social learning is beneficial for learners. Social learning can improve learning and bring positive outcomes. A piece of advice from a fellow student, for example, can help a student perform better and achieve more. Association, collaboration, and conversations help students learn better. Hence, social learning enables students to secure knowledge and helps them relate their knowledge to their life processes.

HOW TO INITIATE SOCIAL LEARNING STRATEGY IN ONLINE TEACHING

1. **Evaluate the zeal of your students to acquire social learning**: This is a significant step as it is wise to initiate social learning to students who are willing to accept it.

2. **Analyze the progress you would want your students to achieve with social learning:** It is important to specify what level of progress social learning would bring to your students. This will help you monitor their progress.

3. **Use social learning platforms:** Choose social learning platforms that enhance improved relationships between students and has great aspects like discussion forums, content curation, access to teachers and instructors, enabling sharing of learning experiences, establishing communities, and encouraging students to participate and increase their knowledge base.

4. **Improve the access to information:** If technology is used efficiently, information can become incredibly easy and quick to access.

5. **Provide and take feedback:** Use the platform to organize feedback sessions from students.

Social learning can be effectively used in cases like group collaboration projects, group discussions, mentoring, problem-solving cases, social surveys and in many other situations.

COOPERATIVE LEARNING

The concept of cooperative learning has been around for a long time. Cooperative learning entails arranging lessons around small factions that function concurrently in a way that the success of every group member depends on the group's success. There are various categories of groups for distinct situations, and they balance some key elements that differentiate cooperative learning from individual learning. Cooperation involves much more than communicating with other students, assisting, or sharing resources with other students, or being physically close. There is a fundamental difference between just putting students into groups and fostering cooperative interdependence among students.

Cooperative learning is based on teamwork. The basic essence of cooperative learning is to bring out the positive impacts of working together while emphasizing the significance of individual obligations. This is common with cooperative learning as students work with each other, but they also have their assignments to do. In this case, students are working in cooperative learning as well as being social. However, working socially can build students' learning experiences and give them mastery and skills on what they do.

Things to note before starting with Cooperative Learning

One of the core values of cooperative learning is to retain students on an assignment. This is where teachers come into play in cooperative learning. When cooperative learning comes up, you are not teaching directly, rather, you're making sure that groups of students stay on assignments. It's easy for students to start interacting when they are given a group assignment to do.

Also, you can also generate a schedule of certain cooperative learning techniques you intend to use with your students. That way, you will always have extra strategies anytime your students complete a task and move to another task. Moreover, once you have those scheduled strategies, you can easily build a cooperative learning plan that makes it incredibly difficult for students to stop focusing.

The Essence of Cooperative Learning

A study has used the same curriculum and examination to compare cooperative learning with conventional class teaching. Students who learn with cooperative learning know relatively more, memorize longer, and acquire better skills than students in conventional learning classes. Students also appreciate the cooperative learning more than conventional learning classes, so they are more likely to give attention to classes and complete assignments.

Students also enjoy engaging in team and group work. Cooperative learning improves students acquire the abilities critical to work on difficult and sophisticated projects in a reasonable amount of time.

Features that make cooperative learning successful

Cooperative learning can be used in a wide range of classroom environments varying from minor to major lectures, as well as in online classes. There are five key factors of cooperative learning that enhance its success.

Accountability — Students must acknowledge accountability for playing their part and enabling the group to reach its learning goals.

Teaching techniques — Students need to cultivate interpersonal abilities to function together positively so teachers can focus on topics and offer assignments about collaboration and teamwork.

Promote communication — Students must work together by giving assistance, credit, and feedback.

Group strategy — Students should strategize on how best to achieve their learning goals.

Positive interdependence — Individual action and group action are essential to the success of the team.

BENEFITS OF COOPERATIVE LEARNING

- Better results and greater accomplishment

- Supporting, and devoted associations

- Boosted cognitive health status, and improved self-esteem

TYPES OF COOPERATIVE LEARNING STRATEGIES

Cooperative learning is a learning strategy that lets students learn through social experiences in the group. The types of cooperative learning are:

1. FORMAL COOPERATIVE LEARNING STRATEGIES

Formal cooperative learning includes putting students in a group for a timeframe of within a few weeks. This entails creating groups by assigning students who work well together, and however have the capacity needed to achieve goals. These are a few formal cooperative learning strategies to attempt:

i. Address unorthodox standards

It's incredibly very easy for deviant group rules to evolve and circulate, group rules constantly change as group members converse with each other, which gives room for terrible routines. For instance, you can teach students how to give a positive response. But if one student starts castigating others, the other group members may copy the attitude. Therefore, to promote effective group learning, you must regulate group activity, spot and address bad norms with solutions. By doing that, students will develop into becoming great supportive and validating group members.

ii. Evaluate group work

Cooperative learning expects easy interaction and effective cooperation between group members, hence evaluating teamwork can motivate students to act properly. Motivate students by evaluating teamwork aspects such as open communication, if they help each other actively, do they give helpful feedback, are they working to complete their assignments. By doing this your students will learn the strategies needed to complete their tasks.

iii. Build confidence

Building confidence teaches the significance of cooperation and responsibility which are the vital factors to the success of a learning group that will last long. Build confidence and trust by introducing trust games. These games are entertaining and they allow group members to unite. Also, you can enhance these games by illustrating fundamental aspects of group work, such as attending actively and contributing actively.

iv.   Use related circumstances

Allowing students to fight the actual problems that affect them, gives them the possibility for engaging in cooperative learning. Most lessons that use this problem-based learning get increased attendance from students and better behaviors from them. This technique increases students' enthusiasm as they collectively unravel related problems. Additionally, this process can be helpful to students who have a hard time understanding abstract reasoning.

2. INFORMAL COOPERATIVE LEARNING STRATEGIES

This method of cooperative learning entails formulating groups working to accomplish a definite learning goal within a time frame of the entire particular lesson.

Informal cooperative learning strategies can include:

i.   Asking diverse questions

Diverse questions are questions with numerous answers that facilitate valuable responses that allow students to learn from each other's viewpoints. An example of a diverse question is "what's the best means to get ready for a science test?" In this case, the result can be an essay, a lab task, or any other ideas that comes up. This way, informal cooperative learning becomes a differentiated teaching strategy and a way to build collaboration skills.

ii.   Use the jigsaw method

This is a well-known technique for many teachers, the jigsaw strategy facilitates a social relationship between groups and gives students a defined function within their team. The method includes splitting a task into subtasks, allocating one to each group partner. Students then work to become specialists in the lessons their subtasks cover. They can also do that through guided study, or maintaining conversations with students from other groups dealing with the same subtask. Then, they exit their actual groups to share recent information. This method educates students on how essential personal participation is to achieving group goals.

iii.   Increase and expand new ideas

This scheme functions particularly well as a means of splitting lengthy presentations.

After the class has initiated a new or intriguing concept, split students into groups. Introduce them to problems for them to analyze and questions to handle the idea. Then, hold a class meeting to submit and observe findings.

3. BASE GROUP COOPERATIVE LEARNING STRATEGIES

These groups last for a prolonged time than the formal cooperative learning teams, as group members assist each other while seeking to achieve driving learning goals over the academic year. The teacher creates groups, plans steady meeting periods, and listing specific plans for students.

Base group cooperative learning strategies include:

i.   Initiate technology that facilitates cooperation and collaboration

Technology boosts group productivity, consider giving them tutorials on:

- **Online brainstorming** — There are websites students can use, to develop open and comprehensive intellectual maps quickly.

- **Cloud-based word processing** — Rather than swapping documents for revisions, and corrections, students can use online word processing tools, such as Microsoft word, libreoffice, openoffice or googledocs to prepare collectively jotted down assignments.

- **Educational games** — There are numerous games concentrated on committing learners and dealing with their difficulty.

ii. APPOINT ROLES

Base groups should have members who oversee particular aspects of the teamwork protocol. For example, a student can negotiate discussions, another can take issues to deal with, and another can submit study outcomes, you can also appoint roles based on expertise on the subject matter. By doing this, you're ensuring that every student participates and plays a meaningful role in enabling each other to achieve learning goals throughout the year.

iii. GIVE A BEFORE- AND AFTER-TASK TEST

The essence of this is to see how well base groups are doing and track their progress, give each student a test before and after working together.

iv. CONSTRAIN SCAFFOLDING

Enable faster student management and accountability by modifying the feedback and scaffolding you provide based on where a base group is in a given project.

Oversee students closely when they commence a project, and give guidance, fill learning gaps, approve additional aids, and avail yourself to respond to questions. Also, as students become familiar with the subject matter and are conveniently operating towards achieving their learning goals, your focus should be to motivate them to introduce new concepts and suggestions, make sure they are performing their roles, allow them to teach themselves. This process will help you attain one of the purposes of cooperative learning which is students successfully being in control of their intellectual growth.

INTEGRATIVE LEARNING

Integrative learning is a strategy of learning where the learner relates previous information and occurrences with new information and occurrences. In this case, students bring out their abilities and relate them to new experiences at a more detailed level. The notion behind integrative learning is that students take control of their own learning pace, become important scrutiny who can make significant relationships between various professions, and utilize meaningful reasoning to virtual problems.

Integrative learning strategies can be used to help students control their learning, pull out their knowledge from past experiences and give the students the chance to relate this knowledge and the information, abilities, and understandings that they have. A logical result of using integrative learning techniques in a course is to enable an increase in engagement for students.

INQUIRY-BASED LEARNING

Inquiry-based learning is a learning strategy that emphasizes the role of a student in the learning process. In this case, students are encouraged to examine the content, ask questions, as well as share opinions and knowledge rather than the teacher telling them what they should know.

Inquiry-based learning uses several strategies for learning, including guided teaching and group conferences. Instead of cramming information, this method encourages students to learn by doing. This enables them to develop understanding and knowledge through analysis, familiar occurrences, and dialogue.

It is a learning and instructional strategy that gives importance to student questions, ideas, understanding, and analyses. Inquiry-based learning concentrates on examining an open question or issue. Inquiry-based teaching focuses on pushing students beyond popular interest in the spheres of integral reasoning and knowledge.

Using methods such as guided analysis, document computation, and question-and-answer sessions, you can operate inquiry activities in the form of case studies, group projects, inquiry projects, and field jobs. You can also give distinct activities to your student which has been modified to your student's field. Whichever activity you use, ensure it allow students to cultivate distinct techniques for unraveling questions.

The key to getting successful and accomplished students is to make sure they are engaged with and connected to any subject they are learning. Although, sometimes, it may be difficult to do because things are easier said than done. For most students, the conventional classroom style of learning makes them bored and lukewarm. And because of that, they aren't actively learning or following the lesson and they barely understand the subject being taught. This is the reason for the introduction of an inquiry-based learning strategy. Just like experiential learning strategy, inquiry-based learning effectively engages and commits students in the process of learning. It allows them to analyze a topic from their own experiences not just listening and jotting down.

THE BENEFITS OF INQUIRY-BASED LEARNING

Inquiry-based teaching helps in developing abilities and proficiency to enable students to attain a higher level of thinking, it provides other benefits such as

1. Enhances Curriculum Content

Inquiry-based learning can be used to enhance an appropriate curriculum content and increase knowledge of important concepts. This is due to curiosity's impact on the brain. When an idea ignites curiosity, there is increased activity in the brain. And when students show more curiosity than usual with regards to a particular subject, relax their brains by managing their questions to initiate an inquiry activity. They should significantly have this important information after you do this.

2. Enhances learning experiences for kids

Learners find sitting in a classroom jotting down notes, and absorbing information, quite boring. Inquiry-based learning improves the learning process by allowing students to analyze and research the subject themselves.

3. Gets the brain ready for learning

An inquiry-based learning approach allows students to explore and share their concepts and opinions about a subject. This helps facilitate their curiosity about the topic and it also educates them on the skills they can use in exploring topics that spark their interests. Operating a quick inquiry activity to begin a lesson helps learners assimilate knowledge easily. Precisely, it's generally known that curiosity readies the brain for learning, so inquiry-based learning ignites curiosity which lets students become more skilled at comprehending and memorizing information and ideas. A simple way to incite interest is by initiating an inquiry activity as a surprise. Then, give students a free question to answer either personally or as a group. This will encourage commencing lessons in a curiosity-inciting, academic, and motivating way.

4. Improves students' comprehension

Students relate better with what they are learning based on their inquiry than barely remembering and cramming information and facts. This enables them to comprehend and understand better than they would and not just keeping and cramming facts.

5. Facilitates a better Understanding of Content

Inquiry-based learning makes students understand topics better. This is because asking and unraveling questions gives students a sense of control. They should be able to develop an understanding of their own.

6. Makes learning a rewarding experience

Inquiry-based learning can encourage students to discover the inherent rewards in learning. Inquiry-based learning demonstrates to students how rewarding exploring can be which lead to a form of learning which motivates students to learn more.

7. Enhancing initiatives and skills

Students can expand and refine their skills through inquiry-based learning. As they analyze a topic, they develop fundamental reasoning skills. The cognitive skills that students develop can be used to improve their initiatives.

8. Creates a passion for learning

Inquiry-based learning is constructed to develop students' passion for learning. When students can absorb the content in their way, they are equipped to gain an increased understanding and they generate a passion for learning.

9. Works in any learning environment

Inquiry-based learning is also advantageous to teachers, as you can redefine the learning style to suit any learning atmosphere. Additionally, you can modify the speed and subject to suit the students' needs, offer students who have difficulty in acquiring knowledge regular classes, use various inquiry methods for difficult activities, improve on ideas that students have shown interest in. By doing this you will have the flexible skill to use inquiry strategies in your classes.

10.   Gives room for differentiated teaching

An inquiry-based learning activity gives you an opportunity to use differentiated teaching strategies, which appeals to the various learning styles of your students. This involves allowing students to work individually, or in a collective manner by grouping them. Since Inquiry in particular generally involves techniques such as discussion, you can also provide information in the form of audios or videos to provide a vast range of topics and means to utilize it. Inquiry learning makes it possible for you to meet up with your students' diverse learning needs and diverse choices.

11.　Gives students a sense of control over their learning

Inquiry-based learning provides the opportunity for students to have a feeling of control over what they learn and how they learn by exploring a subject, allowing them to discuss their ideas and concepts. Rather than instructing them on what they should do and what they should learn, they can learn in a manner that works for them.

12. Improves students' commitment to learning

As an aspect of effective learning, this technique motivates students to fully commit to the learning system, this is achievable by allowing students to analyze and evaluate subjects, relate to their own experiences, and relate their concerns and questions, which makes them able to engage better.

TYPES OF INQUIRY-BASED LEARNING

There are several types of inquiry-based learning, which can be tailored to suit different purposes:

Structured Inquiry

In this case, you give students an open-ended question and a research method. They must use the method to draw up a conclusion that is backed up by facts.

Open Inquiry

In this strategy, you give students a period of time and assistance. They present unique issues that they observe and analyze through their own strategies and methods, and finally, they submit their results for further discussions and elaboration.

Guided Inquiry

In the guided inquiry, you give students an open question. Normally in groups, and they organize a method of analysis and research to reach a conclusion.

Confirmation Inquiry

Here you give students a question, its answer, and the process of getting the answer. All they need to do to construct an inquiry and critical-thinking skills, and also learn how the specific process works. Nevertheless, no matter the type of inquiry-based learning, inquiry-based learning strives to expand the abilities of students to evaluate, access, examine, and process information.

Chapter 5

THE MOTIVATION THEORY

One of the significant elements of online learning is motivation. Motivation is generally embraced by teachers as one of the aspects of online learning that can have a great impact on the rate and success of learning. Motivation is interpreted in several ways by different researchers, but they appear to concur that motivation is what stimulates and guides human behavior. In learning, motivation usually refers to the desires and efforts of students to learn.

Most students are influenced by extrinsic motivators such as graduating, earning high marks in exams and tests, or being able to get better career opportunities when they graduate. These elements can enhance the motivation to learn in students but the actual motivation to learn can be defined as the students' desire to learn and the fulfillment they feel while learning. The hint to motivating students has to do with an inward desire and personal interests.

As an instructor, it's your duty to make sure your students feel connected and committed to learning, as well as being personally interested in their learning progress. Many of the conditions that are beneficial in conventional educational setups also apply to online learning setups. For example, a low student-to-teacher ratio is crucial for the success of an online or offline student. Nevertheless, there are some distinct strategies online teachers can use to encourage learning, and continuously retaining of grown-up students.

To encourage online students, give chances for students to individually relate to the course, make sure they set their own expectations, organize a procedure for them to oversee themselves and track their improvement and performance, encourage them to work together with you on the syllabus, and act as a motivator, instead of an information dispatcher. It's important that students have a sense of control in their own learning, and also that they certainly appreciate the system of learning.

As a trainer, you can encourage this fulfillment by aiming to make your lessons fun and enjoyable, instead of hard and depressing. You can also make the learning process a priority, instead of placing priorities on degrees or competitions in which students compete over who has the highest knowledge.

As a teacher, you should make it one of your objectives to enable active participation by students in online class conversations, give options in terms of research assignments and essays, and give lots of positive feedbacks. This encourages students to stay focused and connected to the class, and other students as well. Some of the reasons why students drop out of online classes is because they feel isolated, deserted, and disconnected, or because of poor participation of the teacher and insufficient communication skills.

Hence, a feeling of communal relationship, communicating with other students, and cooperation are all factors that contribute to the success of online learning. Other factors like eLearning tools, supportive learning atmospheres, and mobile applications can also enhance the success of online learning and make learning feel relatable and applicable to students' real lives. The general idea to succeed in motivating online students is to create motivating conditions and engagement in your course. Nevertheless, do not disregard your major purpose which is to teach the students.

Motivating Grown-up Students

Both online and offline grown-up students become more motivated to learn when they are treated like exceptional people with purposes, objectives, and goals. When they see you as a mentor rather than as a dictator or tyrant, they will be more relaxed and contribute better to the course.

The main purpose is to enhance the grown-up students' inherent degrees of motivation while reducing the emphasis on outside sources of motivation, to help assure students that they are self-reliant and independent. It is beneficial to use a few general administrative and managerial strategies to your online teaching process because online students are usually non-conventional but rather adult students who may have been involved and actively employed and working for some years.

- Avoid dominating, opt instead to motivate them

- Listen and pay attention to them

- Make them accountable and responsible for their actions

- Humanize your course

- Make a dip in their performance a teaching or learning opportunity

- Communicate with them

One of the most practical ways to boost and motivate online students is to relate the subject matter to real-life experiences and familiarities. You can do this in the form of simply starting each day with an online conversation referring to happenings and occurrences in the news to the lecture for that day. Also, you can decide to bring in role-playing by making students connect recent lesson ideas with prospective pursuits or theoretical situations.

Relationships and communication are an important part of the learning system because interacting with others strengthen ideas by enabling students to establish and deliberate key ideas from the lesson or content. These discussions can be done on student discussion forums, discussion boards, and chat rooms. Therefore, making students interact with one another while engaging with the topic.

Another strategy of motivating students is making them feel encouraged by making them track their improvements and performance. A great style you can use in the strategy is the portfolio method. In the portfolio method, students can gather all their tasks into a single folder which will enable them to track their growth and improvement in the learning process. A manual collection would be very useful for online learners so that learning won't feel so digital.

Additionally, make your students evaluate the learning process after they finish every assignment. This gives them a feeling of control of their own learning pace, and they will be able to pinpoint areas where they excel and areas where they are still struggling and get the guidance they need in those areas.

TYPES OF MOTIVATIONS

There are two main types of motivations; intrinsic and extrinsic.

Intrinsic motivation involves a personal behavior done, to feel contentment, fulfillment such as the pleasure of performing a specific action or gratifying one's interest. Intrinsic motivation comes from a feeling to learn for self-gratification or to have a better understanding of the content.

Extrinsic motivation involves behavior done to fulfill some extrinsic conditions or satisfaction. Extrinsic motivation comes from a feeling to succeed for the sake of achieving a goal. Extrinsically motivated students are usually interested in getting grades and ratings while intrinsically motivated students are normally interested in their tasks. It is essential for the online teacher to understand the meaning of the two types of motivation and use them in the teaching process so that students will nurture positive attitudes to learning.

HOW TO MOTIVATE ONLINE STUDENTS

Whether you instruct online or offline, whether you teach kids or adult students. Motivating students will always be tough. Online courses can pose various difficulties over the regular classroom because you don't see them physically. Without a physical presence, vocal cues, hints, and gestures that can get lost. Motivation in online learning is one of the toughest aspects to achieve. It involves an excellent combination of desire and devotion. Know what your online learners require and meet their requirements. True learning can't take place if there is no passion for the student to learn. An online teacher needs to know how to motivate students.

1. Reward Students' Successes

Students are humans who like to be rewarded. Appreciation helps create self-esteem and self-confidence, which in turn, helps motivate students to move on to the next task. Whenever you can, display outstanding and excellent job done by fellow students. Ensure you use different individuals to mix it up. It will give credit to those individuals as well as encourage and motivate the other students to do better. In another context, be detailed and definite when giving negative responses and feedback, but try not to be rude and insulting. Another strategy to reward and motivate students is to give them additional credit upfront. This will encourage them to meet up with deadlines and milestones to get the reward.

2. Create a Supportive, Open, and Accessible Learning Atmosphere

One of the best strategies for engaging students in creating virtual office hours. This makes you available to them. Furthermore, even though you can't see online students, you can make them a part of the class and introduce them to their fellow students and commit them to interact with each other. Learners need to believe that you understand what you do and that you are concerned about them, their progress, and their achievements. Create diverse learning styles for your diverse students because not all of them will want to express and interact, and not all of them will learn in the same manner and pace. So, you can give instances and illustrations, research studies, and several methods of disseminating information about a subject to help meet up with unique strengths, learning behaviors, and interests.

Online classes are remarkably useful because it gives students a choice since students can decide the assessment method they want. Also, to create a supportive environment you should provide rapid feedback on assignments and tasks. This gives you the opportunity to make a connection with your students, therefore encouraging and motivating students to the point where they achieve learning independence. Try to respond to student's concerns and issues within a day. Achieving this facilitates the focus and commitment of the student to the lesson.

Include a positive and helpful feedback on assignments and tasks. Personalized messages about a student's assignment a message that they are valuable. Even if the student has a low grade, useful and constructive feedback from you will be appreciated by them. Craft a weekly message in the form of a text or video message to post to the course home page. Doing so demonstrates to students that the instructor is indeed involved and engaged in the course.

3. Establish Online Groups

Split students into groups and allocate tasks to each of the groups. Give them hints to solve the tasks. They will have the opportunity to review practical findings and explanations with their group members and evaluate every part of the task. This not only reinforces their motivation and gets them effectively involved, but also increases interaction and cooperative skills. Additionally, they profit from the ordeals of their group members and discover things from another perspective.

4. Make Students Track their Development

Several students are self-motivated. However, individuals are different, not every student has self-confidence. These students may need motivation, enthusiasm, and encouragement.

5. Allow mistakes to give rise to learning opportunities

In learning, being successful or unsuccessful plays an important part in the motivational drive of a student. The actions which are beyond their abilities and skills can bring a negative influence on them. Both complete failure and complete success may be demotivating. One of the major barriers for online learners is fear of failure. They aren't encouraged to learn because they are scared of making mistakes. As a consequence, they don't contribute nor partake in the learning system. You can turn errors and mistakes into learning opportunities, thereby eliminating the barriers. Offer your online students the opportunity to evaluate and reexamine their process after every lesson activity, then offer an individualized response and helpful criticism that they can use to establish goals. Choose an Learning Management System (LMS) that helps you cultivate a learning culture that addresses errors and mistakes instead of criticizing them.

6. Give students time for self-reflection

Some classes have a particular level of confusion. Online students are required to maintain learning speed with their counterparts and get the knowledge rapidly, which gives little or no time for evaluating the topic and assimilating the message. This is why it's critical to give time for self-reflection and analysis. Integrate periodic moments where online students can evaluate their processes and point areas that need modification. These moments offer online students the ability to establish a significant connection with the lesson which personalizes their learning experience. It also gives them control over their growth and improvement, which pushes their intrinsic motivation.

7. Encourage friendly competition using leaderboards

Friendly competition that steers online students to achieve success. We all aspire to be better individuals than others. The continuous quest to attain our real potential as humans is a driving force that propels us to become better. Leaderboards can help you gain the leverage of social competition in your learning. Make sure that every online student is on board and allow them to leave because some people don't react well to contest and choose to do it independently.

8. Modify online assignment into serious games

Intense games enable online students to review complicated assignments and procedures. Integrate general game machinists, such as badges and levels, and online activities training tutorials. For example, online learners must demonstrate that they have a certain ability before they can progress to the next level, or finalize the following stage of the process in order to win the "boss". Intense games are stimulating and delightful, which encourages online students to effectively commit to the learning process.

9. Give online students a feeling of control over their learning direction

One of the significant factors of improving online students' motivation is providing a feeling of control. They may not be able to define the learning results or goals. Nonetheless, they can still decide which tasks they accomplish and when they accomplish it. This steers online students to set their objectives and customize their learning process. For example, online students who desire more learning activity can partake in intense games. A great way to achieve this is to ask them a question like what they want to get out of their class, make them suggest lessons while you keep sufficient concept and technique to meet the learning goals, ask for their opinions during lessons about the subject matter.

10. Make the learning environment orderly

Sharp and bold colors make students feel more enthusiastic and propelled. Too many symbols on the screen create a tone of confusion and disturbance which is revealed in their achievement. Assess your learning environment from a personal perspective. How do the color theme and font make you feel? Is the format accomplishing the chosen outcome?

11.   Assist students in Setting Attainable Goals

Assist students in setting attainable goals in the class. You can lay out a calculated actualization duration. By doing that you are eliminating all forms of unrealistic expectation with the exact preparation period. Also, advise students on what they are required to do to accomplish their goals and achieve success. Success is interpreted differently by each student, but by giving them realistic objectives of what you require for different phases of accomplishment, they will work towards meeting up with the desired expectations. Also, ensure you identify the difficulties and challenges that they might encounter and persistently be ready to help them out when they encounter those difficulties.

12. Adopting Appropriate Style of Presentation

A suitable presenting style can boost students' motivation. You should be mindful that the style and method you use to relate the course will have some impact on your students' motivation. For instance, adopting diverse, interesting, and difficult learning tasks that need speeches, reading, paying attention, writing, and reasoning can boost students' motivation to the highest level. Avoid being just an educator but, also, a motivator that encourages and motivates students to learn online. Also, note that talking too much can make a student see your class as boring and uninteresting, so try finding a balance between talking to them and motivating them.

13.   Create a Connection with the Students

A good connection between a teacher and the students is particularly essential. If the students like the teacher, they will like the teaching even if it is offline or online, and they will want to learn from the teacher. This indicates that their enthusiasm and morale for learning would be boosted. On the other hand, if they dislike the teacher, they will not be interested in the teacher's online classes, and even refuse to give attention to or participate in the learning activities. So as an educator and instructor, create a good standard for your students and rapport well with them. A few ways you can rapport with your students is by being their friend, simplifying your instruction to make the class fun, and interesting, being modest, and attending to students equally and appreciating them.

14. Personalizing, Understanding and Recognizing Students

Attending to students by calling their names can motivate and encourage them to be more attentive. When students in the online class feel recognized, their level of motivation will be boosted. You can create a comparable class atmosphere by:

- Taking steps to acknowledge the students knowing and respecting their interests, learning styles, language level. The more you understand them, the easier it will be for you to teach

- Creating a learning atmosphere where students are respected when relating their viewpoints and opinions.

- Inquiring about their beliefs or views. This will empower you with useful information to establish and schedule forthcoming activities and also can motivate the students. Enabling students to bring their ideas and concepts in the learning process is one of the important ways to increase students' motivation.

Chapter 6

EMBRACING DIGITAL TECHNOLOGY

The importance of technology in education is unquestionably the capacity and the demand to reach more students. Though most people prefer to depend on conventional ways of education, the opportunities that technology brings are unlimited. To name a few, access to information and learning has relatively become easier as a result, including a wide range of learning styles and choices. The cost of education has considerably diminished, with available options like online classes and by removing the desire to purchase manual learning books.

Students no longer need to join a full-time program to learn from the best schools. You can easily download contents right to your phone, which makes the learning process both easily accessible and transferable. Education has become increasingly flexible. Technology has broken down barriers of location and time. Technology facilitates how instructors do their duties, giving helpful and beneficial ways to develop a relationship between teacher and student. Free educational learning devices accessible online has increased the accessibility of education around the world. You can completely obtain a fully accredited bachelor's or master's degree online and in some cases, tuition-free.

Apart from access to knowledge, information, and data, new technology can certainly fascinate and endow students. Since so many youngsters are technologically aware, make use of iPads and other forms of smartphones, learning through technological classes will possibly become more exciting than discouraging. Ever since the involvement of technology in education, expanded opportunities became available and accessible for both teachers and students in the online environment. Today's teachers are presently challenged with a decision of knowing the best online educating technology available to them.

Here are the fundamental standards and measures to analyze before fully engaging in a platform.

Scaling

The most competent instructors around the globe will most likely be the most famous. The question is, does a technological, educational framework permit learners to gain access to the teachers and instructors with a large student base? If not, there is no distinction between a traditional classroom and an online one. An education technology platform should be able to let students gain access to the teacher no matter how famous the teacher is. Furthermore, learners have preferences of the best instructors anywhere on the globe, so these instructors gain access to the students through the platforms they are already aware of and have been using before. Online classrooms through the use of technology platforms should be able to effortlessly take numerous students, and give them equal access to the knowledge at a lower cost.

Accessible

A technology platform should be able to maintain a video experience, operate through the general online setting, have few behind lags, and minimize data loss, and be accessible to everyone.

Compatibility

New technology may be exciting and thrilling but it will often depend on the technology that is around it. A good technology platform should be friendly and compatible with the present industry. It must be able to allow you to fully incorporate the good visual, audio, and data streaming services into a teaching platform. Students should be able to connect with teachers using platforms they already know and are familiar with. The visual streaming service is very significant because many academic schemes rely on high-quality video streams so that students can read from the screen.

THE USE OF ONLINE LEARNING TOOLS

It's tough to give an exact definition of online learning tools, because of the differences in tools variety. But you need to simply understand online learning tools apply to any scheme, app, or technology that reinforces the ability of a teacher to deliver lessons and the ability of that student to access that information. Online tools are tools you can access through the Internet. With the sudden rise of technology over the years, Students' and teachers' thinking has changed too. Nowadays, a pretorial of online tools can enhance your capacity to convey recent and fresh information to students, while giving them several options for learning information and outcomes. You may be able to instruct more vigorously and your students will appreciate learning more by utilizing these varieties of tools. Online tools for learning will not take your place as the teacher. Instead, they provide distinct alternatives to tutor in various manners that aren't likely in conventional classrooms. But it will improve and strengthen your lessons instead of replacing your teachers.

TYPES OF ONLINE LEARNING TOOLS

Online learning tools are categorized into online classrooms, assistive technology, and apps.

ONLINE CLASSROOMS

Students have accepted and now satisfied with using the Internet to get facts and information about diverse subject matters unknown to them. Decades ago, you would have to go to the library before you can get information but presently it' different. Nowadays, we just take our phones and ask Google to give us any information we desire to know. It is for this purpose many students desire to foster their learning instead of going to school and staying to learn at the pace of the teacher.

There are three fundamental kinds of online classrooms that you should be familiar with in fulfilling your students' learning requirements.

Flipped Classrooms

A flipped classroom comprises a class where students are entirely accountable for learning before going to the physical classroom. Students utilize online student-facilitated learning in this case. Operations and activities are done in the class directed by the instructor with the belief that students have previously understood the online assigned content.

Blended Classrooms

Blended classrooms consist of a physical classroom with an instructor with some online student-facilitated learning, utilizing the online tools and assistance that a teacher keeps and arranges for the students to use.

Distance Education Classrooms

Distance education classes can also be called virtual schools. It consists of 100 percent of teaching using the internet and online tools. In this type of classroom, the educator and the learner would not see each other and would not be associated with the same physical environment.

ASSISTIVE TECHNOLOGY

One of the incredible things about online learning tools is their capacity to easily make learners with bodily challenges and cognitive learning challenges reachable. Assistive technology tools are commonly already formulated programs and may barely have a need for quick easy practice on how to use it. Examples are

Text-to-speech Programs: Several programs have text-to-speech attributes that helps slow and struggling readers by reading the written word loud to their hearing.

Proofreading programs: Proofreading programs have been built-in to make tasks and duties easier

APPS AND WEBSITES

1. WeVideo

The Wevideo is a great unified website that enables you to put together videos as a group in your class. It blends videos of the entire group and gives a feeling of oneness that is somewhat difficult to achieve when you're doing distance learning.

2. WordPress.org

Online projects are usually difficult to do together. Use the WordPress.org to create a website with the association that you can all relate to. This displays your knowledge and potential out there for the world to see.

3. A.nnotate

Explore A.nnotate. It has incredible functionality with an extensive range of alternatives and choices. It is a great option if you're operating with individuals who like exploring functionalities on the internet and can handle things sophisticated procedures.

4. Scribble

Scribble isn't so sophisticated. It's a simple learning tool that's fit for a vast range of students. They can share information and notes, combine ideas, and complete work on projects, which will give them a sense of togetherness.

5. Dropbox

Dropbox is a popular essential tool that makes it easy to share files, organize general folders where students can upload their files, build links where students can pick the class schemes and so much more.

6. Prezi

Prezi is what you need for great presentation, it's spontaneous, looks fabulous, and allows you to create beautiful presentations. Check it out as it's great for both teachers and students' presentations.

7. Edmodo

Edmodo is an educational tool that unites students and teachers and is absorbed into a social system. In this tool, instructors can formulate online cooperative groups, manage and deliver academic contents, measure student performance, and discuss with parents, among other functions. Edmodo has over 34 million users who use it to create a learning process that is more enhancing, individualized, takes advantage of the opportunities generated by technology.

8. Socrative

Socrative is formulated by a group of entrepreneurs and individuals who love education, Socrative is a system that enables instructors to develop activities cities or educational games which students can analyze using smartphones, laptops, or tablets. The teachers can see the outcomes of the tasks and, may revise other lessons so they can be more personalized.

9. Projeqt

Projeqt is an online learning tool that enables you to generate multimedia presentations, with active slides where you can add interactive maps, links, online quizzes, Twitter timelines, and videos, among other alternatives.

10.   Thinglink

Thinglink enables instructors to develop informative images with music, sounds, texts, and pictures. These can be conveyed on other websites or social networks, such as Twitter and Facebook. Thinglink provides the opportunity for teachers to develop learning procedures that stimulate the interest of students through interactive and informative content that can broaden their understanding.

11.   TED-Ed

TED-Ed is an educational learning platform that permits developing educational classes with the collaboration of teachers, students, animators, and any other person who wants to boost knowledge. It helps teachers and students to get access to information and have active participation in the process of learning.

12.   ClassDojo

ClassDojo is a tool used to enhance student behavior, teachers give their students timely feedback so that a good attitude in class is 'rewarded' with grades and students have a more willing attitude to the learning process. ClassDojo gives real-time notifications and messages. The data that is accumulated about the student learning attitude can be conveyed to parents later using the net.

13.   eduClipper

This framework permits teachers and students to share and analyze quotations, sources, and educational content. In eduClipper, you can take information from the internet and then share it with the group members, which provides the opportunity to organize the educational content found online more effectively, develop methods of analysis, and keep a digital record of what students acquired during the lectures. Furthermore, it gives a chance for teachers to establish a virtual class with their students and creates a folder to save all the tasks and activities carried out.

14.   Storybird

Storybird strives to use storytelling to facilitate writing and reading skills in students. With this tool, teachers can use an easy and simple interface to develop interactive books online. The stories created can be sent by email, and published, among other alternatives, and added to blogs. In Storybird, teachers can also formulate projects and tasks with students, give timely feedback, and manage lessons and grades.

15.   Animoto

Animoto is a digital tool that enables you to create high-quality videos within a short duration using any smartphone or device. It encourages students and assists them in boosting educational classes. The Animoto interface is helpful and useful, enabling teachers to develop audiovisual content that adjusts to the various educational needs of students.

16.   Kahoot!

Kahoot! is an educational platform that includes games and questions. With this tool, teachers can organize questionnaires, discussions, or surveys that support academic lessons. The content is brought to the classroom, while playing and learning, the questions are responded to by students. Kahoot! facilitates learning that is based on a game that improves student commitment to the learning process and establishes a unique, friendly, and pleasant learning atmosphere.

THE BEST ONLINE TEACHING PLATFORMS

The fate of learning lies in artificial intelligence. Visualize you having a virtual instructor that communicates with you in a personalized way. It knows your desires and gives you precisely what you require until you become a master in your desired subject matter. It is completely encouraging, engaging, and personalized. However, some intelligent systems monitor the cognitive operations of a student while figuring out a problem and analyze the learner's knowledge of the subject, already but AI is not mainstream yet. Sooner or later it will become so. Meanwhile, there are some popular platforms available that teaching and learning flexible, accessible, and convenient.

Note that online teaching is beginning to become a considerable source of earnings for a vast range of people all over the globe because it has some considerable advantages over the conventional schooling in terms of having a flexible working time, more options to reach more students, simple communication tools and re-usable online materials. These platforms also encourage human interaction and social learning which are important aspects of learning and some of these platforms below seem to emphasize that in their doctrine of learning & teaching.

Udemy: Udemy believes in changing the educational system by enabling everyone to learn from its collection of more than 20000 Subject Matter Experts. To a relatively vast extent, Udemy has been growing in its goal. This online learning platform has several content creations tools such as PDF documents, PowerPoint, text and video content that can be put together to develop and launch courses. Udemy online training platform can be used by instructors freely. However, Udemy earns its' revenue by receiving 50% per sale of a course. Udemy has over 12 million students.

Teachable: Teachable which was previously known as Fedora, is a teaching platform where you can develop and sell your online courses. It enables you to create your course content using different media tools to customize and name your course (e.g. logo, color, and styles) and launch it. The platform then takes care of the rest that include benefits such as learner analytics and course earnings. Presently, teachable has over 3 million students, 7,500 instructors, and 20,000 courses. The figures are going higher and higher. Teachable offers a free eBook to attract customers, this eBook vividly explains aspects such as course creation, video creation, slide presentation, etc.

Eliademy: Just like Udemy, Eliademy operates as a market area for online courses from languages to technology. It has an LMS-like learning setting with all the aspects such as tasks, quizzes, discussions, learner analytics, and grading.

Podia: Podia is a fairly new platform among others and it is beautifully designed. You can organize your courses, digital downloads, customers, e-mail subscribers, payments, and data in one spot, which is precisely what an online course designer would want. What makes it a little distinct from others is that you can develop downloads either to sell it or give it away as lead magnets. This can assist you in expanding an audience more effortlessly and get new customers for your online courses.

Thinkific: Thinkific is a simple online course platform. You can put all your content together, include quizzes and surveys, give certificates of completion, monitor learner progress, and incorporate third-party tools through Zapier. One of the useful aspects of Thinkific is its continuous product development. They also take feedback from users and modify the platform, including new features all the time. It's an amazing platform for over 35000 content developers who are looking to name and sell courses. If you are trying to increase your audience rapidly, you should try using Thinkific. Thinkific is a high-class exception. Teachers have little or no difficulty in creating, publishing, scaling, and marketing their courses.

WizIQ: WizIQ is also another common platform in the eLearning system. For all purposes and intentions, this online teaching software has been the platform instructors use to do live and on-demand webinars. It provides adequate features such as slides, desktop sharing tools, audio, video, etc. WizIQ is very common among educational course content developers. It's very easy to develop courses and launch them on WizIQ online platform.

www.openlearning.com: You can develop your course content and teach your course through this simple and friendly platform. Social engagement among learners is very crucial in this platform.

www.helphub.com: This is an online teaching website that directly connects teachers and students over online messaging and calls. It is further possible to have group learning meetings. It looks like an easy means of teaching and learning. Users ask their questions and get responses from teachers. It is also interesting as that you can notice the teachers who are online and start chatting with them directly.

Ruzuku: Ruzuku is another useful addition to eLearning platforms. Instructors aren't expected to have vast technical know-how to use this platform. Moreover, Ruzuku puts in tremendous actions to make it simple for Subject Matter Experts to develop and launch courses. It has a lot of great provisions such as PayPal payment gateway, everyday backups, MailChimp integrations and many other useful features.

www.learnworlds.com: This platform is enticing and fascinating because it provides you with an e-book creator, interactive video tool, and a chance of networking for learners. It also makes use of gaming to even encourage them more. It is relatively strong in terms of marketing options, content authoring, and interactive tools for social learning.

www.coursecraft.net: This platform is slightly different from other platforms in the perception that it converts blogs into e-courses. It is practically entirely text and image-based. It can serve as an option to conventional online courses for those who contemplate offering non-academic courses.

Educadium: Educadium is on a driving purpose to help entrepreneurs and associations of all sizes to establish, administer, and gain from online teaching and training through its EasyCampus platform. It has an abundance of features and provisions which from course designing to course publishing.

www.vedantu.com: Vedantu is an online teaching website founded and mainly used in India and other nearby regions. It is a platform where anybody else can teach anything with the use of live video meetings with a whiteboard for visual assistance.

www.bibo.com.ph: This platform is exclusively used for teaching English online. It appears to be relatively enticing to those who might want to contemplate working from home and earn additional earnings. It is a Japanese-established online English teaching service based in the Philippines, which seeks to relate learners and teachers from different parts of the world. Perhaps you may never have thought of teaching online before, but you will be surprised when you learn the world of online teaching and the opportunities it offers.

LearnWorlds: Are you looking for a platform that can complete course content with extensive social learning and increased interaction? Take a glance at the spectacular features of LearnWorlds. The platform's premium positioning has been surprising all these years. There are many remarkable features such as tools to build sales pages, simulators, intelligent sales engine, advanced analytics, and many other features that merit premium positioning. LearnWorlds is a very great option.

Academy of Mine: As the name suggests, the Academy of Mine allows you to start your own online academy. This online teaching software is power-packed with an incredibly organized system. The learning curve is somewhat steep so, if you can go up the curve, you can take advantage of all its strong and vital features.

CourseCraft: If you have it in mind to convert your blog into a profitable business? Then try using CourseCraft. Its editor is adjustable, easy, and sharp enough to create different types of courses. It's integrated with Stripe and PayPal payment processors. Creating quizzes, lessons, and forums. Teachers can generate deals and offers. Students can work together with friends and teachers. It has wonderful custom branding features.

Skillshare: The teachers on Skillshare make as much as $40,000 yearly. Nearly every course lesson involves two key features —video and class project. Lessons are made up of a cycle of small videos whose interval is typically anywhere between 10 and 25 minutes. Skillshare's subscription model is unique and distinct from that of Udemy. Udemy sells subscriptions of private courses while Skillshare sells subscriptions to all its extensive content.

CHAPTER 7

COURSE DESIGN AND DEVELOPMENT

Teaching in an online environment can be tedious even for experienced online instructors especially when they have to prepare a new course. However, with a few easy techniques, the procedure can be relaxing and delightful. These are strategies that any educator can use to ease the stress involved in the process of designing an online course successfully.

1. INVOLVE THE LEARNER

A general misconception is that online classes instruct students to simply glance at or watch videos, and then playback the content in an assignment, essay, or discussion platform. However, this is untrue because multiple activities commit and engage online students. Students should affirm their comprehension of the content as well as improve their engagement with the content throughout any class.

Instructors can integrate and merge certain activities that compare real-world scenarios with theoretical knowledge. Actual activities can range from evaluating and analyzing case studies to formulating problem-based settings where the students can study the problem and generate solutions or deal with voids within the problem.

Instructors also can use inquiry-based learning which requires students to research, examine, and analyze the questions they have concerning the subject matter. A strategy that online instructors can execute to establish inquiry-based learning is through the implementation of knowledge charts. Utilizing knowledge charts can prompt exploration and examination of the content as students recognize what they understand and what they want to understand about the subject. Inquiry commences when students explore the parts that they are not familiar with and create questions to direct them in this research.

2. Ensure cooperation

After incorporating students' involvement in the course and with the instructor, the next phase is to improve teamwork and collaboration between peers. Sometimes, instructors feel that teamwork and cooperation in an online environment are difficult or challenging. However, through the use of easy strategies, cooperation and teamwork can be an easy and useful process in course design. One process is the enforcement of Professional Learning Communities (PLC), which are groups of students who team up and cooperate regularly using emails, discussion forums, video chats, and group phone calls to figure out issues or subject matter associated with the content. Instructors can appoint roles within the PLC to help with the active contribution of all students.

Positions can include facilitator who acts as the team leader and the liaison between the group and instructor, interpreter whose role will be to present contents already leant based on their understanding of the content, reminder whose job will be to restate assignment conditions and deadlines, then you can have a guide or mentor whose responsibility will be to examine team tasks and give professional commentary before submission.

PLCs are helpful in cooperating with credible activities and helping with team scaffolding to enable students who are reluctant and hesitant to partake and contribute. If instructors choose to use group tasks not associated with PLCs, they should give clear and defined intentions and expectations. Before starting the assignment, groups should decide who will oversee the assignment and specify when every aspect will be finished. Instructors can give a map that shows milestones of the assignment, to support students so that they can choose a particular area where they feel confident enough to make contributions. The group will jointly analyze each member's suggestion to form a final product. Students can use developing technology mechanisms such as wikis, blogs, and podcasts to further collaborate.

3. Establish a Clear, Obvious and Stable Structure

The course's design can be deliberately enticing, deliberately uninviting, unintentionally persuading, or unintentionally not enticing. Most times instructors possess tons of concepts and information that are jammed into the online learning platform, which can create a non-persuading learning environment. To be able to create an intentionally persuading and enticing online environment, courses should have a precise, obvious, and stable structure that offers automatic direction and navigating. Each module should have a similar structure with the others.

The direction of reading materials, assignments, tasks, collaborative opportunities should be in the same section and layout. Additionally, each section should have the same looks and layouts with the previous modules and include revised content and learning findings. When doing course design and usage for students, an effective approach is to make sure that all materials used throughout the course are included in the LMS. The course design can play a big role in usage and student success.

One technique for engaging students is through the incorporation of microlearning, which is a trend in online learning. Microlearning involves delivering content through arbitrated micro levels so students are exposed to little learning units on short-term assignments. Microlearning is based on H.A. Simon's 1974 study that highlights the usefulness of building learning experiences that short-term memory can keep. This process summarizes online course designing through the use of a learning module. Planning backward is a practical method to develop a learning module. Instructors can look at all the subjects they want to work on, and then spot the thematic piece of information. The thematic piece then becomes components or learning packs that are a short-term approach to long-term planning.

Within the learning module, instructors give tasks, assignments, and supplemental resources, and tools to reinforce mastery of content.

An effective strategy for module improvement is to start with a summary page that highlights all readings, tasks, and assignments required for the module, also with the due dates for each item. Depending on the LMS, instructors can hyperlink info in the summary page directly to the assignments, which gives a clean and standardized feel to the course. The summary page adds to the course's structure and can help keep students engaged in the learning process and increase academic quality. It is essential to have detailed instructions for all parts of learning points within the learning modules.

Electronic Performance Support Systems (EPSS) can improve students' performances. An example of EPSS within the online learning environment is the use of job aids, which offer an overview of the method or a checklist of how to perform and finish a task. Job aids lessen blunders and errors and likely follow-up questions because they give clear performance goals and correct common misunderstandings and misconceptions. Assignments that expect students to perform a particular task can comprise a job aid to improve student success. Along with job aids, headings posted with each task also indicates available communication and expectations. Students can effortlessly read the assignment information and still not understand what is expected; headings give extra transparency. Students are more successful in assignments when can they are able to precisely predict what to expect in an assignment grading.

4. Reflect, Evaluate and Review

According to educational study and excellence in teaching narratives, a reflective educator is a successful educator. There are several methods that instructors can use to exercise reflective strategies to enhance the learning environment for students. Successful educational course design requires a performance assessment process that has flexible policies. One assessment framework is ADDIE, which has five aspects that are the foundation of course designs, this include:

- Analyze

- Design

- Develop

- Implement

- Evaluate

Reflective instructors use the assessment level to review their courses by using best practices. A few means of reviewing course designs are through student feedback and by maintaining a design note that come up during a semester. Lastly, there are course design titles, such as from Quality Matters, which can assess the course design. In contrast to a conventional physical course, the improvement of an online course is a team effort joining the subject of several or a course writer with the instruction, products, and specialized expertise of a learning design team that consists of learning designers, multimedia specialists, programmers, technical editors. The course author is someone who performs as the content specialist, bringing knowledge of the subject matter and practical learning strategies to the project. The learning designer, who serves as the main tool of communication with the learning design team, gives mastery in course design and development, especially in an online learning platform.

GUIDELINES IN DESIGNING AN ONLINE COURSE

- Appreciate and use the instructional design process in developing your online course.

- Work within a schedule and meet up with declared deadlines. This implies that during the first semester of development, an entire half of the course (including evaluations and tasks) is complete. However, by the end of the first semester of development, all of the content (excluding the assessments and activities) should be finished.

- Collaborate effectively with a learning design team in the creation of the online course.

- Generate course materials and activities that analyze the needs of adults and distance learners while meeting up the needs of conventional students.

- Be interested in sharing ideas, concepts, and cooperating with others.

- Acquire wonderful written and verbal skills.

- Develop the ability to express in a conversational tone with an active voice (vibrant, engaging, and containing humor in appropriate places).

- Appreciate the time and energy needed to develop online course materials.

- Have the zeal to learn and incorporate learning strategies to make content more interesting and useful.

- Effectively formulate course objectives and clarify concepts, principles, procedures, etc.

- Accept feedback, constructive and helpful criticism, new suggestions, ideas, and concept.

- Accept computer-based technology and be ready to learn about new technologies.

- Acquire excellent organizational skills.

- Manage time effectively, meet up with scheduled and stated deadlines, and develop a finished course within the specified duration.

- Be self-motivated with a strong commitment and engagement in researching new ideas and trying new options.

- Acknowledge applicable accessibility, plagiarism, and copyright guidelines.

THE STANDARD COURSE DEVELOPMENT PROCESS

The First Semester

The first semester is used to create the unprocessed and unedited content for the course, or part of the lessons with their related activities and purposes, or all of the classes without the activities or assessments. During that duration, the course author usually meets with the learning designer, to first blueprint the course layout and assessment strategy, and then later to examine the content that the author has drafted. The message that is conveyed in these initial meetings is contained in the New Course Questionnaire.

The learning designer also works with the author to formulate a course development plan that highlights milestone decisions for each segment of the course development process. These initial meetings acquaint the course author to the online course development process. The learning designer is also acquainted with the course by reviewing the syllabus and any other related course content. When suitable, the course author, with the aid of the learning designer, consumes time getting the technical, administrative, and pedagogical strategies necessary to establish, and teach in a distance learning environment. They are also acquainted with the challenges involved in preparing and teaching a course online.

Course authors are allowed access to a variety of examples, templates, and other resources for use during course design and development. Once the author(s) and the learning designer have had a few meetings to deliberate the course, one of the first tasks for the author(s) is to get the course Blueprint. The essence of the blueprint is to reveal to the learning designer the author's feelings and opinions on the extensive agenda for the course (thereby making sure that everyone is on an same page).

The plan deals with what will be covered in the course, the general materials that students may need for the course, and information about course goals, purpose, objectives, course requirements, the overall course structure, the lessons, and topics. This is identical to a course proposal that is prepared for University approval, but it is more detailed. The document is like a great conversation piece for the author and designer to utilize while creating the online course. It also instructs the learning designer of the different skills and creativity that will be required to improve the online course materials so additional team members (e.g., programmers and multimedia specialists) can be brought in to the project as the process is ongoing.

Subsequently, the writer will create a sample lesson using any strategy he or she prefers. For some writers, this can be in the form of a Word document. For others, they can record their lessons in audio form and then have it transcribed to provide the author with the unprocessed content that he or she can then revise. Still, others might already be competent in authoring contents in an online environment and might choose to instantly design content and bypass some of the previous steps.

With a sample lesson, the learning designer will then take the material and work with the other members of the learning design team to design an online model of the lesson. As the team works through the blueprint content and puts it into its online form, the learning designer will include comments, questions, and suggestions relating to the course content, learning activities, and assessment strategies. "Marked-up" course materials are then shared with the course author for review and revision. This is generally a repetitive process, with team members swapping materials and doing modifications and corrections numerous times as items are completed.

Once both the author and designer are okay with the final model, the author can then begin to draft another lesson. The same give-and-take process is used between the author and the learning design team to place the additional lessons online, mark them up, and make any important corrections and modifications until they are satisfied with the result. Ideally, by the end of the first semester, the course author should have developed half of the foundation of the course content, which includes all student learning activities and evaluation strategies.

The Second Semester

In the second semester of the development process, the learning design team completes the course content and begin to either start focusing on the second half of the lessons or the developing and incorporating of student learning activities and evaluation strategies into the course. They will also complete the other aspects of the course website, including the online syllabus and course orientation. While several conditions contribute to the success (or failure) of a project, a team development strategy requires good communication among the team members to make sure that things work well. How that interaction takes place varies from team to team, and it's based on the choices of the group. The point is not in how interaction takes place, but rather regularly. Once a course has been designed and prepared for registration, the development process is not yet completed. Each course goes through several stages of constructive and summative assessment. Slight modifications are usually made each semester, and extensive revisions are planned as well, at a duration that varies depending on course content. The actual development team generally supports the course writer in all course modifications and corrections.

Phases and Activities

The course design and development method are informed by a standardized instructional design process and the academic expertise of instructional developers. Generally, the framework used to support course design is a revised edition of the instructional design model ADDIE (Analysis, Design, Development, Implementation, Evaluation). The following phases and activities are included in the course design and development process:

Planning and Analysis

The planning and analysis phase allows the course designer and DLPDS to examine the needs and requirements of the students and the course, and to create a decided timeline for completing the work. The following are some of the activities involved in this phase:

- Project kick-off meeting

- Orientation to the course design process

- Confirmation of a schedule of dates

- NEEDS assessment

- Risk assessment

- Creative discussion

- Copyright considerations

- Design

Proper instructional design is the bedrock of a high-quality online course. During the design phase, the DLPDS team up with the designer to create a structure for the course and formulate and align results alongside assessments. These activities include:

- Writing the outcome of the course

- Defining the structure of the course

- Determining the evaluation strategies

- Writing the unit outcomes

- Defining the unit structure

Development

In the development phase, the course designer creates and prepares the materials to be used in the course. The DLPDS gives support and feedback as the content is designed and refined. The following are some of the activities involved in this phase:

- Media Development: Develop custom media (i.e., video, learning objects, etc.)

- Content Development: Write content storyboards, develop any supporting instructional content

- Revise instructional design

- Review content storyboards

Implementation

In the implementation phase, the Teaching & Learning Technologies team works to develop a course website in the learning administrative system. These steps include:

- Integrating media and content into CourseLink

- Developing web pages with consideration of accessibility guidelines

Quality Assurance

A quality assurance analysis is conducted once the course website has been established. The activities involved in this phase include:

- Instructional design review

- Course developer review

- Technical review

- Completion of all revisions

Evaluation

Once the course has been offered, it is crucial to collect feedback so that any necessary modifications and revisions can be done. This phase includes:

- Conducting a course evaluation

- Conducting a learner feedback survey on course

Project Timelines

The aspects of course development such as developing media, writing content and securing copyright permissions, take a considerable amount of time to complete. As well, the team needs to contemplate the accessibility prerequisites of course and web materials, quality assurance criteria, and best practices in online learning.

CONCLUSION

Online courses are becoming an increasing form of education preferred by individuals for courses that may not be possible to attend in normal traditional colleges which is why there will always exist an opportunity for those who make the effort to ensure that they deliver value to their course attendees.

Take advantage of the effective online teaching strategies outlined in this book will help you ensure that you are accessible to your students and that you can design appropriate teaching methods that can facilitate better student success.

By using the active communication techniques appropriate in engaging students, your students will be more receptive to your course, have a positive attitude, and stay disciplined throughout the course duration.

The cognitive and social strategies discussed in this book really work and should not be underestimated when you apply them. The benefits are almost very easy to see as soon as you start applying them.

The apps and websites listed here are by no means exhaustive as new ones keep added every day. Those tools aim to make your work of managing your online course a lot easier.